# FIRST-PERSON STORIES OF THE KENNEDY ASSASSINATION

BY NICOLE HORNING



ROSEN PUBLISHING PRIMARY SOURCE LIBRARY

ROSEN PUBLISHING

Published in 2027 by The Rosen Publishing Group, Inc.
2544 Clinton Street, Buffalo, NY 14224



Designer: Deanna Lepovich
Editor: Nicole Horning

Cataloging-in-Publication Data

Names: Horning, Nicole.
Title: First-person stories of the Kennedy assassination / Nicole Horning.
Description: Buffalo, NY : Rosen Publishing, 2027. | Series: The Rosen Publishing primary source library | Includes glossary and index.
Identifiers: ISBN 9781725342958 (pbk.) | ISBN 9781725342965 (library bound) | ISBN 9781725342972 (ebook)
Subjects: LCSH: Kennedy, John F. (John Fitzgerald), 1917-1963–Assassination–Juvenile literature. | United States–History–1961-1969–Juvenile literature.
Classification: LCC E842.9 H67 2027 | DDC 973.922–dc23



*Manufactured in the United States of America*

CPSIA Compliance Information: Batch #CSRYA27. For further information, contact Rosen Publishing at 1-800-237-9932.

# CONTENTS

# FOREWORD

History is so much more than just a boring collection of names and dates. It is a collection of stories—sometimes tragic stories, sometimes heroic stories, sometimes romantic stories, sometimes scary stories. And they're all stories of real people who lived real lives.

Those stories can get lost in the shuffle of memorizing battles, studying maps, and listing important court cases or rulers. That's why primary sources are so valuable. They remind us that historical events happened to and because of real people. Reading diaries, looking at photographs, and seeing newspaper articles are just some ways to make history feel personal through primary sources.

Another way is through watching or listening to interviews with people who lived through major historical events. That's what you're invited to do in this book—and all the books that are part of the *Rosen Publishing Primary Source Library*. Each chapter includes quotes from an interview with a real person who experienced a major historical event in a deeply personal way. You can also scan the QR code included at the beginning of each chapter to watch a video interview with the person featured in that chapter.

Created in partnership with Generations Broadcasting, the *Rosen Publishing Primary Source Library* was created to remind readers that there is power in sharing our stories. First-person stories make history come alive. And when history comes alive, we're better able to learn from it—and avoid the mistakes of the past.

The events you're living through today will be part of the next generation's history lessons. As you read and watch the stories collected here, think about what you want your story to be.

*Note: More interviews about the topics featured in this series, as well as many other historical events, can be accessed via a subscription to Rosen Publishing's GBC Stories Database: rosendigital.com/GBCStories/.*

# HOW TO WATCH THE INTERVIEWS FEATURED IN THIS BOOK

- Use your phone's camera, and hold it over the QR code.
- Click the link that appears.
- Watch the video that pops up. If you would like to read a transcript of the interview while you watch, you can click on that option in the video player.

# INTRODUCTION

Some historical events seem to stop time and are so shocking that people remember them forever. The assassination of President John F. Kennedy (often simply known as "JFK"), who was shot by Lee Harvey Oswald, and the later shooting of Oswald as well, are two of those events. Even today, people remember where they were, what they were doing, and how they felt when they heard the news of the events that unraveled during this time.

Kennedy was the youngest elected president in United States history at the time of his presidency. He connected with younger voters and was seen as a symbol of change and possibility in the middle of global tension and fear. He looked and sounded different from earlier presidents, and because he was the first president that many Americans watched regularly on TV, many people felt that they "knew" him.

John F. Kennedy became president in 1961, which was during the Cold War (1947–1991). This was when the United States and Soviet Union were competing for power around the world, and it ended with the **dissolution** of the Soviet Union in 1991. Americans worried that the disagreements between the countries could turn into a nuclear war, and with the Cuban Missile Crisis in 1962, these fears didn't seem too far off. During worldwide crises, Americans often look to the president for leadership and reassurance, and Kennedy's calm personality and confident speeches made people feel reassured.

Kennedy also encouraged people, especially young people, to play an active role in democracy and to take responsibility for improving the world around them. For example, in his 1961 inaugural address, he famously said, "Ask not what your country can do for you; ask what you can do for your country," which made many Americans feel like Kennedy was speaking directly to them.

However, on November 22, 1963, while riding in a motorcade through Dallas, Texas, President Kennedy was shot and died the same day from his injuries. The news spread quickly through radio and television broadcasts, leaving many Americans feeling uncertain about what the future would hold.

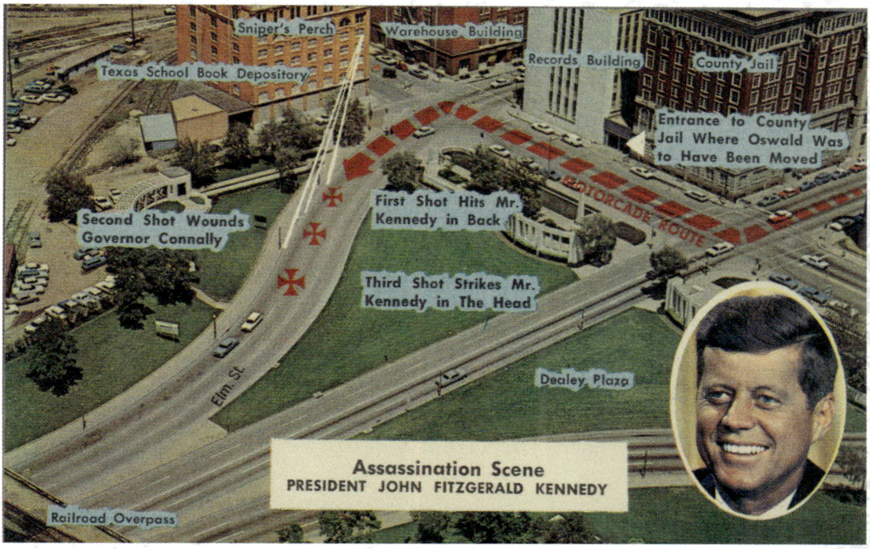


**This photo shows Kennedy's motorcade route, buildings in the Dealey Plaza area, and where Kennedy was on the road when he was shot.**

When Lee Harvey Oswald, the man who assassinated Kennedy, was then murdered himself on live television, the nation was left with even more questions, confusion, and fear.

While the assassination of a young president shocked the nation in itself, it was worsened by the fact that it happened in the daytime and in public, in front of cameras and crowds. Many people were worried that the assassination might be part of something larger, such as a foreign threat. Because of this, schools closed and businesses shut down across the United States.

For many people, the assassination of John F. Kennedy became a moment they'd never forget. Years later, the aura of tragedy surrounding the Kennedys continued when the late president's son, John F. Kennedy Jr., died in 1999 in a plane crash. When this happened, many Americans were again reminded of the earlier loss and the Kennedy family's history of tragedy.

CHAPTER ONE

# BEFORE THE ASSASSINATION

John F. Kennedy wasn't like any president Americans had seen before. At just 43 years old, he was the youngest president in United States history when he was elected. He was energetic, connected with younger people, and seemed more approachable than the presidents that came before. In addition to that, before running for president, he was elected to the House of Representatives three times and the U.S. Senate twice. Kennedy often appeared at public events and on television, making people feel like they really knew him.

In an interview, Jim discussed meeting Kennedy, how he was different, and the impact of his assassination.

## KENNEDY'S PUBLIC IMAGE AND THE 1960 ELECTION

Even before he became president, Kennedy made an impression on people. Jim was a student at the University of Notre Dame in Illinois at the time, and he remembered meeting Kennedy when he was a U.S. Senator:

*I had met President Kennedy when I was a senior at Notre Dame ... He was a junior senator at the time, and I was on the committee to welcome him*

**Scan this QR code to watch Jim talk about meeting John F. Kennedy and later hearing the news of his assassination.**

**John F. Kennedy was a young, energetic president who many people admired. He was also the nation's first Catholic president.**

*when he came ... This guy gets off the plane with no staff, no nothing. It's middle of winter, and he doesn't have a hat on. He just really struck you when you got your first viewpoint of him ...*

*They told [him] he was going to go to a reception of trustees that evening. They have dinner with him. I remember he asked Father Hesberg [if] the students [were] invited. Father Hesberg said, "No, they weren't."*

*And he said, "I want you to arrange for me to have breakfast with the student committee here, and I don't want anybody from the administration." So the next morning, of course, we all showed up at the Morris Inn with our little* Profiles in Courage *book to get it autographed. He sat for about two and a half hours and talked about politics and giving back. The guy had a fantastic attitude. And then he explained how he was going to capture the [presidential] nomination in 1960, which he did.*

Kennedy's accessibility, charisma, and intelligence helped him stand out, and as Jim saw, many Americans felt a

**John F. Kennedy is shown here campaigning in Florida in 1960.**

personal connection to him before he even became president. This connection was critical in the upcoming presidential election against Republican Richard Nixon, because it ended up being one of the closest elections in U.S. history. Kennedy had the support of younger voters and Catholic voters, and the economic downturn from 1957 to 1958 hurt the Republican party. Kennedy's confidence in televised speeches also appealed to first-time voters and led to a shift in American politics.

**FAST FACT**

**KENNEDY WON THE POPULAR VOTE BY 0.17 PERCENT AND THE ELECTORAL COLLEGE 303–219.**

**Kennedy is shown here being told about the Cuban Missile Crisis.**

## AN INSPIRING BOOK

In 1956, Kennedy published *Profiles in Courage*, which won a Pulitzer Prize for Biography in 1957. Kennedy was inspired to write the book after taking a leave of absence from the Senate in 1954 for back surgery. While recovering, he studied the concept of political courage and what it means for elected officials to stand up for what they believe in, even when it seems risky.

In *Profiles in Courage*, Kennedy focused on eight senators who made difficult decisions that went against popular opinion, personal interests, or pressures from interest groups and **constituents**. The senators often lost political support, ended their careers, or faced **criticism** after doing what they believed was right. He explained that courage is about bravery in dramatic moments as well as making hard choices, especially when the effects are immediate.

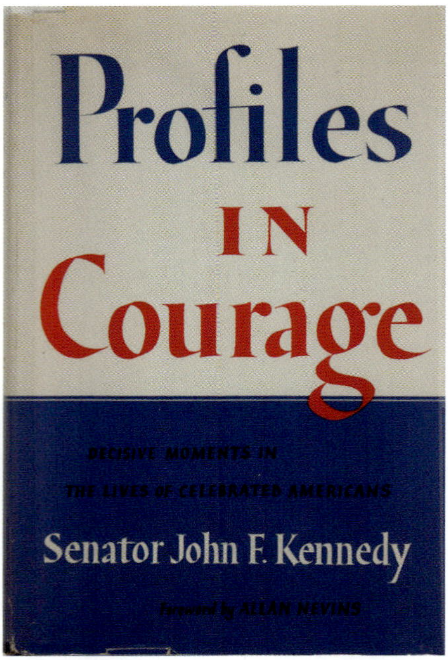

**Kennedy's *Profiles in Courage* is shown here.**

The book especially appealed to young people because it showed that people could make a difference through responsibility and **integrity**. It encouraged them to think about leadership as a service and connected with Kennedy's own ideas about leadership, which prioritized duty, sacrifice, and commitment to the greater good.

## THE COLD WAR

Kennedy became president during a tense period of the Cold War. The United States and Soviet Union were competing for influence across the world, and ordinary Americans worried that a small mistake beyond their control could lead to a nuclear war. One of Kennedy's biggest challenges came in 1962, during the Cuban Missile Crisis. Jim discussed the challenges Kennedy faced at the time:

> *When I was transferred down to Albuquerque [New Mexico], we made hydrogen bombs ... About 1962, when the Cuban Missile Crisis happened, we were considered a prime target ... They're broadcasting a ship is coming up to the demarcation line ... I can remember thinking at the time, 'Man, that's [a lot of] responsibility to place on one guy, what's he going to do?' And of course after the ship turned around and left, once again, I had admiration for the guy.*

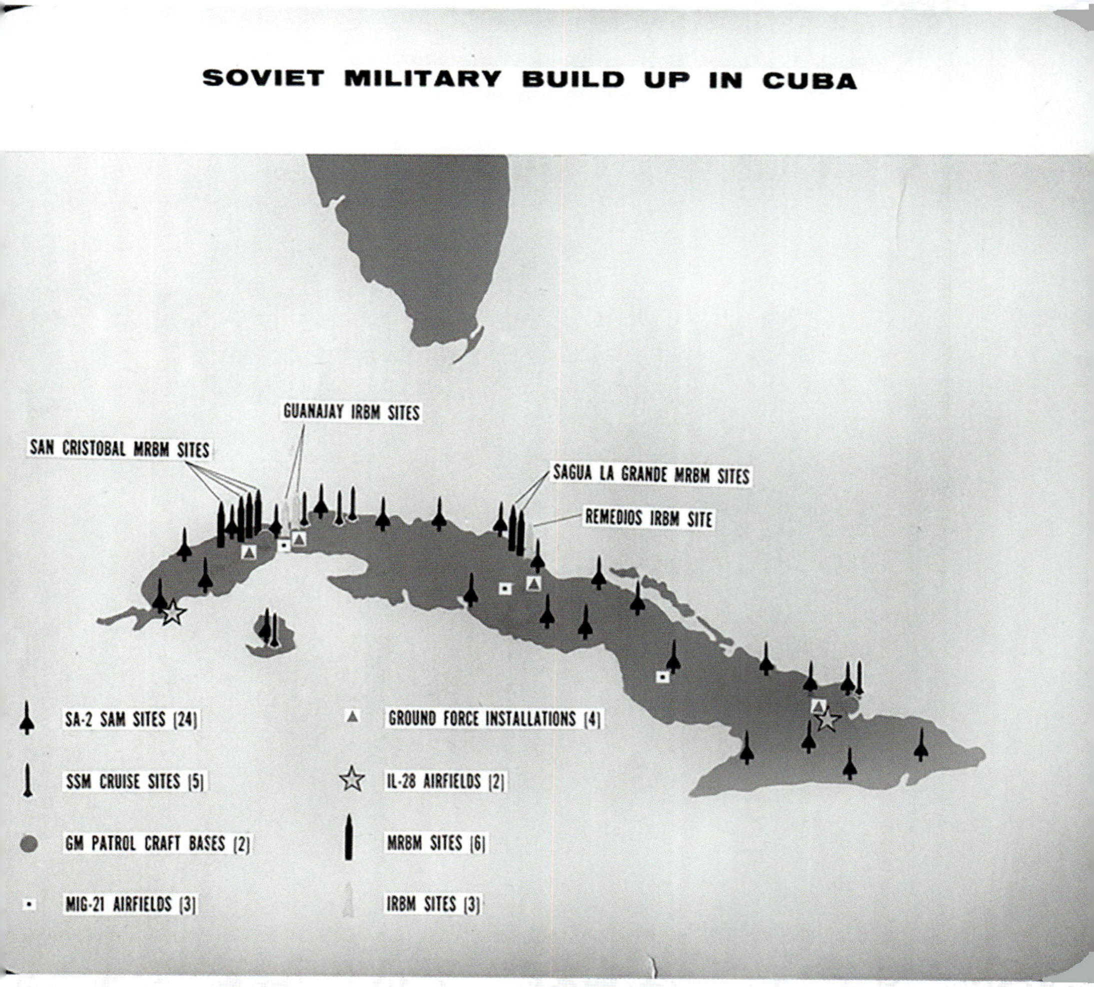


**A map of the Soviet military presence in Cuba during the Cuban Missile Crisis is shown here.**

The Cuban Missile Crisis was a 13-day standoff between the United States and Soviet Union. The Soviet Union had placed nuclear missiles in Cuba and threatened major U.S. cities. Kennedy responded by ordering a naval blockade of Cuba. The Soviets then agreed to remove the missiles, but only if the United States removed its missiles from Türkiye.

This was an important moment in Kennedy's presidency because it was the closest the United States came to nuclear war during the Cold War and Kennedy successfully balanced **diplomacy** and military pressure. His ability to remain calm during the crisis showed Americans that he could handle high-stakes situations.

After the Cuban Missile Crisis, many people felt reassured that the worst dangers of the Cold War were over. However, in November 1963, the next crisis came from within the United States itself.

**When the Kennedys arrived in Dallas in 1963, they smiled, shook hands, and greeted people. At this time, security wasn't as much of a concern. The assassination changed that.**

## NOVEMBER 1963

In November 1963, Kennedy was traveling to Texas to build political support for his re-election and to address tensions within the Democratic Party between Governor John B. Connally and Senator Ralph Yarborough. To show unity and help mend the feud, Kennedy was going to tour the state with both men. The trip was planned for maximum exposure, so it was a multi-city tour that included Fort Worth, San Antonio, Austin, Houston, and Dallas.

**FAST FACT**

**KENNEDY WAS THE FOURTH U.S. PRESIDENT TO BE ASSASSINATED IN OFFICE. THE OTHERS WERE ABRAHAM LINCOLN, JAMES GARFIELD, AND WILLIAM MCKINLEY.**

The Texas trip was a routine political tour that was carefully planned. However, it ended up becoming one of the most shocking events in American history. Jim was one of many Americans who learned about the assassination while going about his daily life. He said:

> *I had been assigned to a task force. Part of the job of the task force was to visit some of the other locations of the Atomic Energy Commission ... One of the locations we went to was an assembly plant where they ... made the bomb. And they took us to the igloos where they assembled these things. These igloos were down below ground, and when we got finished, we came up out of the igloo and we got into the car, and all of a sudden two Jeeps closed in on us and said, "Get out of the car." And they had guns and it was really kind of serious.*
>
> *And I said, "Well, you know, what is going on?" And they said, "Didn't you know that President Kennedy was assassinated today?" It just hit you like a ton of bricks.*

## LIFE COMES TO A HALT

After learning of the assassination, Jim still felt uncertain about what was happening and what it meant:

**Lee Harvey Oswald, shown here, is the man who murdered Kennedy.**

> *They finished searching us and everything, and they said, "You can go." They didn't know what was happening. They didn't know whether there was a Russian attack or sabotage or what was going to happen.*

As the news spread, daily life came to a halt. Jim had previously made plans with his brothers to go to the Notre Dame game in Des Moines, Iowa, the next day. But when he arrived there, he found that the town was very quiet and everything was shut down. Movies were canceled, stores were closed, and the Notre Dame game ended up being canceled as well. Jim said:

> *I went out for a walk. I walked past the cathedral and I went in and I sat in the pew and I thought about meeting John Kennedy and how much I really admired the guy ... You're overcome with grief. He wasn't a personal friend, [but I] felt bad for his wife and kids. I know they say that 80 percent of Americans felt physical*

*discomfort that day. I did. It hit you.*

Like many others in America, Jim and his family were watching coverage of the Kennedy assassination on TV when they saw another significant event occur:

**FAST FACT**

**KENNEDY HAD 64 LIVE PRESS CONFERENCES THROUGHOUT HIS PRESIDENCY, FOR AN AVERAGE OF 1 EVERY 16 DAYS.**

*We were sitting at the breakfast table; I remember looking over at the television. They were bringing Oswald through the downstairs of the Dallas Police Department. And all of a sudden this guy jumps out and shoots him ... It was just mind boggling.*

After these events, people felt symptoms of extreme stress such as headaches, sleeplessness, and dizziness, and there was even an increase in heart attacks. Part of the reason why so many people felt this kind of reaction to the

**The murder of Lee Harvey Oswald was captured in this photo.**

**The Kennedys were a young family who were admired by many people. John and Jacqueline are shown here with their children.**

assassination was because of the immediate and constant television coverage, which essentially brought the tragedy into the homes of Americans. Additionally, Kennedy was the first president to have unedited televised speeches, and with the frequency of them, he had become a familiar presence in people's homes, leading to people feeling like someone they personally knew had died.

## HOW YOU SEE HISTORY

1. How did television affect the way Americans experienced Kennedy's presidency and assassination?
2. Why do you think so many people felt a personal connection to Kennedy, even if they had never met him?
3. Why did the assassination cause so much confusion and fear across the country?

CHAPTER TWO

# THE DAY UNFOLDS

November 22, 1963, was carefully planned. It was the second day of Kennedy's multicity tour to build political support, and he had a schedule full of speeches, a public breakfast, a luncheon at the Dallas Trade Mart, and a motorcade throughout Dallas. All of these appearances were designed to connect with voters on a more personal level. In an interview, David describes being at the Dallas Trade Mart with his wife that day, where he was waiting to attend the president's luncheon.

## THE TRIP TO TEXAS

The trip to Texas was important for Kennedy's political strategy to gain support for his re-election. The **itinerary** was just two days long but covered five cities. On the first day, November 21, Air Force One arrived in San Antonio, and John F. Kennedy and his wife, First Lady Jacqueline Kennedy, went in a motorcade throughout the city. Then, they flew to Houston for another motorcade and then to Fort Worth, where they spent the night. Crowds gathered at each stop, eager to see the president as his wife, who had rarely joined him on political trips in the months before the assassination.

On the morning of November 22, Kennedy spoke to

**Scan this QR code to watch David discuss being at Kennedy's luncheon the day of the assassination.**

**The Kennedys are shown here departing Air Force One at Love Field.**

## FAST FACT

THE MOTORCADE ROUTE THROUGH DALLAS WAS PUBLISHED IN LOCAL NEWSPAPERS AHEAD OF TIME, SO PEOPLE KNEW WHERE TO STAND. HOWEVER, IT ALSO PROVIDED OSWALD WITH CRITICAL INFORMATION FOR PLANNING THE ASSASSINATION.

a large crowd in Fort Worth then went to a breakfast for the Chamber of Commerce. The Kennedys then departed Fort Worth for Dallas. When their plane landed at Love Field, there was a large crowd waiting. The president smiled and waved as he and the First Lady greeted supporters and shook their hands. They were joined by Texas Governor John Connally and his wife,

**The Kennedys are shown here arriving at Love Field and greeting the public on November 22, 1963.**

Nellie Connally, who would ride with them in the motorcade through Dallas.

The motorcade route was planned to go through downtown Dallas streets so as many people as possible could see the president. To allow a clear view, the Kennedys were in an open top car driving at a slow pace to make it easier for people to wave, cheer, and take photographs. The motorcade was supposed to last about 45 minutes and was 10 miles (16 km) long. It was to end at the Dallas Trade Mart, where Kennedy would deliver a speech at a luncheon.

## THE DALLAS TRADE MART

While the motorcade moved through Dallas, many people were already at the Dallas Trade Mart, waiting for Kennedy to arrive. In

**Motorcades are a common way for leaders to travel.**

David's interview, he remembered waiting at the Trade Mart with his wife and hearing the news of the assassination:

> *My wife was asked to sing "The Star-Spangled Banner" at the luncheon for Kennedy at the Dallas Trade Mart ... [We] were given four choice seats close to the head table. We were told by Eric Johnson, who was the master of ceremonies and later mayor of Dallas, that the luncheon was being delayed because the motorcade was delayed. But finally he said, "Go ahead and*

*eat." So we had just probably taken the first two or three bites of our luncheon, and the press corps came in and sat down at the tables, just a short distance from where my wife and I and another couple that we had invited to go with us were sitting. And they had barely sat down, and one reporter ... had a transistor radio, and he jumped up and said, "My God, the president's been shot."*

## FAST FACT

**SCHOOLS DISMISSED STUDENTS EARLY ON THE DAY OF KENNEDY'S ASSASSINATION. LESSONS IMMEDIATELY STOPPED, AND TEACHERS TOLD STUDENTS DIRECTLY IN THEIR CLASSROOMS OR OVER THE PA SYSTEMS. MANY STUDENTS AND TEACHERS WERE CRYING OVER THE NEWS.**

The planned luncheon never happened. People were in shock, and at the time, it was unknown whether the president was alive. David said:

**Oswald shot Kennedy from the sixth floor of the Texas School Book Depository, shown here.**

*It was just an overwhelming experience. So we never finished the lunch ... [People] were crying. They were concerned. Was there a conspiracy? Who was behind all this? That was before Oswald was captured. People just, wherever they were, not only at the Trade Mart but throughout America, just stopped working and went back home or went to pick up their kids at school. Schools closed.*

## THE ASSASSINATION

Kennedy's murderer was 24-year-old Lee Harvey Oswald. He was a former U.S. Marine, and had **defected** to the Soviet Union for a while. In January 1963, he ordered a revolver, a rifle, and a telescopic sight through the mail, which would later be used in the assassination. In October 1963, he moved to Dallas, where he started a job at the Texas School Book Depository. On the day of Kennedy's assassination, he went to the sixth floor of that building, in Dealey Plaza,

**Oswald shot Kennedy from this corner window of the Texas School Book Depository.**

**The Kennedys are shown here moments before John F. Kennedy was shot. Governor Connally and his wife are in the middle row of the vehicle.**

and fired three shots at 12:30 p.m. Two bullets hit John F. Kennedy, with one entering his neck and the other entering his head, and he slumped toward the First Lady. The other bullet wounded Governor Connally, hitting him in the back.

Kennedy was rushed to Parkland Memorial Hospital, which was just a few minutes away, but nothing could be done to save him. He was pronounced dead at 1:00 p.m., just a half hour after being shot.

Oswald immediately fled the scene to go back to his rooming house but was stopped along the way by Patrolman J.D. Tippit. Tippit believed that Oswald matched the description of the suspect, who was already being described on police radio. At about 1:15 p.m., Oswald also killed Tippit. At 1:45 p.m., Oswald was **seized** by police in the Texas Theatre. On November 23 at 1:30 p.m., he was **arraigned** for the murder of President Kennedy.

In 1962 he returned to the U.S.

In August this year he passed out pro-Castro leaflets on a New Orleans street.

On Sept. 26 President Kennedy

motorcade route.

**On Oct. 14** he rented a room in Dallas.

Friday Oswald was seen by R. S. Truly and a Dallas policeman

of the firm, superintende standing in at 411 Elm started.

# Suspect Captured In Movie Theater

"I protest this police brutality," cried President Kennedy's suspected assassin as police dragged him from the darkened Texas Theater in Oak Cliff Friday afternoon.

A crowd of several hundred pressed forward, chanting, "Kill the S.O.B.!"

Had not officers moved quickly and with authority, 24-year-old Lee Harvey Oswald might have suffered a worse fate than the world leader he is suspected of killing.

Mrs. Julie Postal of 2728 Seevers, cashier at the theater at 231 W. Jefferson, had called police shortly before 2 p.m. and reported "a strange-acting man."

She had been told by a shoe store manager that a man had been ducking in and out of stores as police sirens wailed in the area. She was told the man had run into the theater.

"I really don't remember if I saw him go in or not," she said, "but apparently this man was running from the police for something. I had been listening about President Kennedy's death and was so shook up I couldn't notice much of anything."

When Mrs. Postal realized that the man said to be inside was probably the culprit the police were searching for, she told the shoe store man and an employe of the theater to "look around in there."

They couldn't find anyone, but as they passed the back section of the middle aisle downstairs, they heard a seat snap or crack.

About this time police—only a few blocks away at the scene of the shooting of Policeman J. D. Tippit at 400 E. Jefferson—surged en masse into the theater.

"Watch him, he's armed," shouted ne detective. "I'll get that SOB if he's in there," replied another.

Minutes later three policemen dragged the screaming, kicking ex-Marine out.

Police tried to put one of their caps over the man's face and another held his mouth shut as they piled him in an unmarked police car. Five policemen went along.

The crowd was angry, but the scene had switched too fast for it to act.

Officer M. N. McDonald was the officer who said he disarmed

# Warren Lays Shots To Bigotry

WASHINGTON (AP)—Chief Justice Earl Warren said Friday President Kennedy was assassinated "as a result of the hatred and bitterness that has been in-

Mrs. Mar Oswald, h President Friday ni guerite O The suspe her daugh mitted to

*STILL H*

**A newspaper article announcing the capture of Lee Harvey Oswald is shown here.**

However, Oswald's arrest didn't bring relief or clear answers. Instead, people remained tense as they followed every update on the TV and radio. Because the news was broadcast live and continuously, many people saw the events unfold in real time, which had rarely happened before.

On November 24, Oswald was being transferred from his jail cell to an

## FAST FACT

JOHN F. KENNEDY DIED AT PARKLAND MEMORIAL HOSPITAL ON NOVEMBER 22. HIS MURDERER, LEE HARVEY OSWALD, DIED AT THE SAME HOSPITAL ON NOVEMBER 24. OSWALD'S MURDERER ALSO DIED AT THIS HOSPITAL IN JANUARY 1967 OF COMPLICATIONS FROM CANCER.

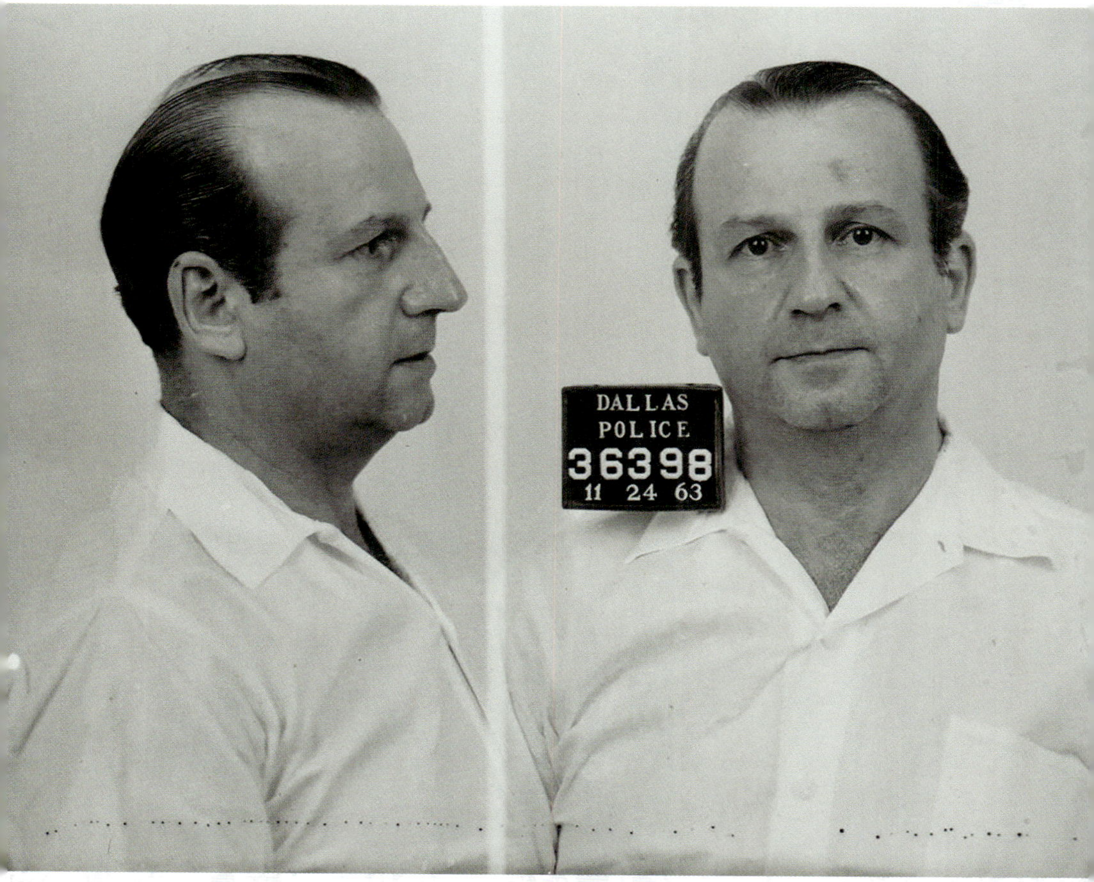


**Jack Ruby, shown here in his mugshot, killed Lee Harvey Oswald shortly after Oswald killed Kennedy.**

# CONSPIRACY THEORIES AND THE KENNEDY ASSASSINATION

A conspiracy theory is a belief that an influential organization, group, or individual is secretly responsible for an event, often without clear proof. The assassination of John F. Kennedy is one of those events that has led to many conspiracy theories, making it one of the most debated events in U.S. history.

One of the most well-known theories involves the "grassy knoll," which was a small hill in Dealey Plaza near where Kennedy was shot. Some witnesses say they heard shots from that direction, leading to claims that there was a second shooter in addition to Oswald.

These theories came about largely because there was a lot of confusion right after the assassination. News reports **contradicted** each other, details changed rapidly, and people were trying to make sense of the event. The fact that Oswald himself was killed two days later on live television added to the public's suspicion and removed the chance for a full trial. Additionally, Oswald denied killing Kennedy, saying he was being framed and he hadn't shot anyone. Oswald never confessed to killing Kennedy before he was shot by Jack Ruby.

The Cold War also played a part in these theories. Many Americans feared foreign enemies, especially the Soviet Union, and wondered if the assassination was part of a larger plot. And because Kennedy was young, popular, and admired, it was difficult for people to believe that one person could have done this.

Multiple investigations found that Oswald acted alone. However, unanswered questions have allowed these theories to continue, even to this day.

**The grassy knoll, shown here, is part of one of the most popular conspiracy theories surrounding the assassination.**

**After John F. Kennedy's assassination, newspapers and magazines published special issues such as these remembering his life.**

interrogation office. The moment was broadcast on live TV, so people saw in real time when a Dallas nightclub owner, Jack Ruby, shot Oswald. Ruby's stated reason for killing Oswald was grief and anger over the assassination, and he also wanted to spare Jacqueline Kennedy from going through the trial. Oswald died that same day at Parkland Memorial Hospital in Dallas.

## HOW YOU SEE HISTORY

1. Why do you think theories about Kennedy's assassination continue to interest people so many decades after it happened?
2. What role does the media play in shaping the public's opinion during shocking events?
3. How did people's reaction to the assassination show the emotional impact a leader can have on a nation?

# CHAPTER THREE

# THE TRANSFER OF POWER

Even in times of crisis, the government must continue functioning. One of the responsibilities of a vice president is to step into the role of the presidency if anything should happen to the president. After the assassination of John F. Kennedy, leadership needed to ensure that the presidency continued without interruption, so Vice President Lyndon B. Johnson was sworn in as president. In an interview, Peter discussed the assassination and his mother's connection to Judge Sarah Hughes, who swore in Johnson.

## KENNEDY'S SUCCESSOR

Vice President Lyndon B. Johnson had many years of experience between the House of Representatives and the Senate. Before becoming Kennedy's vice president, he was the Senate Majority Leader. This experience gave him the background needed to steer the government in times of crisis, but he wasn't as visible to the public as Kennedy had been.

The U.S. Constitution states that presidential leadership must transfer immediately to preserve the function of the government. Johnson had traveled to Texas with Kennedy

**Scan this QR code to watch Peter talk about his mother's luncheon with John F. Kennedy and the judge who swore in Lyndon B. Johnson.**

and was in the car behind him in the motorcade, so he was there to step into leadership of the United States without delay.

After being pronounced dead at Parkland Memorial Hospital, Kennedy's body was taken to Love Field and put on Air Force One. At 2:38 p.m. on November 22, Johnson was sworn in as president. Jacqueline Kennedy stood next to him as he was sworn in, still wearing the pink dress she had worn in the

## FAST FACT

JACQUELINE KENNEDY REFUSED TO TAKE OFF THE PINK SUIT STAINED WITH HER HUSBAND'S BLOOD FOR THE SWEARING IN OF JOHNSON. SHE SAID SHE DID THIS BECAUSE SHE WANTED PEOPLE TO SEE WHAT THEY DID TO HIM. THE SUIT HAS NEVER BEEN CLEANED AND WAS TO BE HIDDEN IN THE NATIONAL ARCHIVES FOR 100 YEARS TO AVOID CAUSING THE FAMILY MORE PAIN.

**John F. Kennedy's casket is shown here being transferred to Air Force One shortly before Lyndon B. Johnson is sworn in as president.**

Kennedy was supposed to have a luncheon at the Dallas Trade Mart. This building is part of the same complex as the Trade Mart.

**Jacqueline Kennedy is shown to the left of Lyndon B. Johnson during the swearing-in ceremony on board Air Force One.**

motorcade, which was covered in her husband's blood.

Johnson was sworn in by Texas Judge Sarah Hughes, whom he chose because she was a close personal friend. She was also very close to Love Field because she was at the Trade Mart waiting for Kennedy to show for the luncheon.

## FAST FACT

JUDGE SARAH HUGHES WAS THE FIRST WOMAN TO SWEAR IN A U.S. PRESIDENT.

In an interview, Peter discussed his mother waiting for Kennedy at the luncheon with Hughes:

> *[Kennedy] was on his way to speak at the Trade Mart and my mother was sitting with Judge Sarah Hughes waiting for Kennedy to show up. The U.S. Marshals came to Judge Hughes and told her to go home, and my mother found out*

## "THE BEAST"

Presidential transports have changed a lot since Kennedy's assassination. Heavily armored cars are now common, and with each president, the cars get even more technologically advanced. In 2001, with President George W. Bush's armored transport, the cars started to be called "the Beast."

The presidential armored limo weighs almost 20,000 pounds (9,071.8 kg) and is made of several layers of aluminum, steel, ceramic, and composite armor. It's said that the doors are as heavy as those on a Boeing 757 airplane. The windows are made of bullet-resistant glass that's about 5 inches (12.7 cm) thick, and the tires are made of military-grade rubber. The tires can keep rolling even if they're punctured. The main part of the limo is also sealed against biological and chemical attacks. Inside of the limo is an emergency supply of oxygen and packages of the president's blood type.

Not every single detail of the Beast is known, and this is on purpose to protect the president. Only a very small amount of government officials know every detail. What is known are the few facts outlined above and that it's designed to look normal but provide heavy protection. The Secret Service also has **decoy** vehicles, which look exactly like the president's car so that no one knows which vehicle actually has the president. Once a vehicle is retired, it is completely destroyed so that the construction secrets are kept safe.

*about the assassination. Judge Hughes called my mother about 30 minutes before she swore in Lyndon Johnson, and said, "Turn on the TV in 30 minutes."*

*And actually, my brother shook Kennedy's hand that morning ... I remember I was taking a test at [school] when he was shot.*

## CHANGES IN PRESIDENTIAL SECURITY

Even though Kennedy was the fourth president to be assassinated, presidential security still looked a lot different than it does today. In his interview, Peter discussed his brother being able to shake Kennedy's hand, saying:

**Today, presidents now travel in armored cars such as the one shown here.**

*Anybody that could go to Love Field at the time, and if you were close enough, you got to shake his hand. They didn't have such great security back in the 1960s, and I think that changed a lot after that.*

Before Kennedy's assassination, presidential security was limited. Secret Service agents provided protection during events, but the

## FAST FACT

ONE OF THE WITNESSES OF THE ASSASSINATION WAS A 14-YEAR-OLD BOY WHO SAID HE SAW KENNEDY'S FACE GO BLANK AT 12:30 P.M., WHEN HE WAS SHOT. THE BOY ALSO SAID HE HEARD JACQUELINE KENNEDY SHOUT, "GOD, OH GOD, NO!"

**protocols** were a lot less **stringent** than they are today. Back then, it was common for presidents to **mingle** with the crowds and engage directly with the public. While this created opportunities for personal connection, it also made presidents more vulnerable.

Kennedy's assassination exposed weaknesses in the system. After his death, the Secret Service started maintaining closer **proximity** to the president at events, created more structured procedures for motorcades, improved crowd control and security at events, and perhaps most importantly, **eliminated** open-top cars. Now, presidents travel in heavily armored, sealed, and technologically advanced vehicles. Additionally, Secret Service members work together with local law enforcement to ensure buildings where the president will be are safe and secured, threats are checked along the route ahead of time, and rapid-response teams are utilized.

## HOW YOU SEE HISTORY

1. Why do you think the United States ensures there is a clear and immediate transfer of power after a president dies while in office?
2. Why do you think governments typically change rules only after a crisis has happened rather than before?
3. How might witnessing a sudden change in leadership affect people's trust in the government or their sense of security?

# CHAPTER FOUR

# THE WORLD REACTS

The assassination impacted daily life for everyone across the United States, especially in Dallas. Many people feared that this was just the beginning of a larger attack, and at the same time, Dallas became the focus of national attention and criticism. For nearly 20 years after the assassination, Dallas was known as the "City of Hate" and suffered a severe drop in tourism. In an interview, Pat and Alvie described what it was like in the Dallas area after the assassination.

## IMMEDIATE LOCKDOWNS

Within hours of the assassination, Dallas changed dramatically. Police officers flooded the streets, and buildings and streets were locked down. Alvie was in the hospital with pneumonia when he learned that Kennedy had been shot. He immediately called Pat to tell her the news. Pat said:

> *He phoned me and said, "Have you got the television on?" And I said, "As a matter of fact, I don't." And he told me that Kennedy was shot ... The city just got locked down so quickly ... Nobody could believe it.*

**Scan this QR code to watch Pat and Alvie talk about reactions to the assassination and how difficult it was in Dallas.**

**Jacqueline Kennedy and her children, Caroline and John Jr., are shown here leaving the funeral ceremony.**

## FAST FACT

ABOUT 250,000 PEOPLE SHOWED UP TO PAY THEIR RESPECTS TO KENNEDY AS HE LAY IN STATE IN THE CAPITOL ROTUNDA. TENS OF THOUSANDS OF PEOPLE HAD TO BE TURNED AWAY, SOME OF WHOM HAD WAITED ALL NIGHT OUTSIDE IN THE FREEZING RAIN. THE LINE TO PAY RESPECTS WENT ON FOR MORE THAN 2 MILES (3.2 KM).

Roads closed, and police stopped cars, telling people to go back home. The speed of the response showed how uncertain officials were about what might happen next. Even people who weren't near downtown Dallas felt the effects as movement across the city became limited.

## "CITY OF HATE"

As shock of the assassination spread across the nation, Dallas quickly became a focus of national anger and blame, while Dallas citizens were **traumatized** because this tragedy happened in their city. Even before the assassination, Dallas had started developing a certain **reputation**. Many people in the city held extreme right-wing conservative views, and news outlets didn't hide their dislike of

**Kennedy's casket laid in repose in the White House. Thousands came to pay their respects, and members of the military stood guard.**

# THE ZAPRUDER FILM

On November 22, Dallas businessman Abraham Zapruder caught one of the most famous pieces of film footage in history. He was filming Kennedy's motorcade with his 8 mm home movie camera at the same time the shots rang out in Dealey Plaza. His film captured the assassination in real time, frame by frame. The entire video lasts about 26 seconds.

The Zapruder film became very important to understanding what happened during the assassination. It showed Kennedy's reaction to the shots, the movement of the motorcade, Jacqueline Kennedy jumping onto the back of the car to reach for pieces of Kennedy's skull, and Secret Service Agent Clint Hill climbing onto the back of the car. It is the only film known to exist that shows all of the assassination; however, there were about 31 other people in Dealey Plaza who are known to have photographed or filmed at or around the time of the shooting.

At first, the film was private, but it was soon shared with news outlets and became widely known. It's also been central to many

**The Zapruder film was filmed on this 8 mm camera.**

Kennedy. Even before the assassination, Dallas was starting to be known as a "City of Hate."

Even though it was one person who killed Kennedy, the entire city of Dallas was seen as responsible in the nation's eyes. Today, while there is a memorial for Kennedy in the Texas School Book Depository, other memorials in the area are rare. Residents also conspiracy theories. For example, people say that the direction of Kennedy's head suggests that the shot came from the front, where the grassy knoll was, instead of behind Kennedy, where the Texas School Book Depository was. Additionally, there is a woman in the film who many believe also caught footage of the assassination. However, if she did capture footage, it has never been released or was **confiscated** by law enforcement.

Today, the Zapruder film is preserved as a historical **artifact**. In 1998, it was **acquired** by the U.S. government and moved to a cold-storage vault belonging to the National Archives.

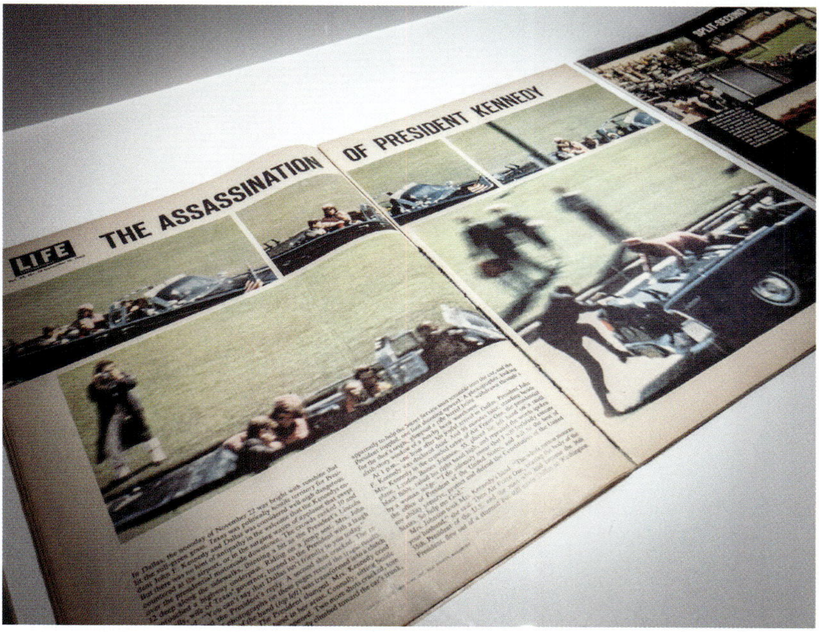


***Life* magazine bought the Zapruder film and published photo stills in the magazine, which are shown here.**

state that spray-painted Xs will randomly pop up on the road where Kennedy was shot because conspiracy theorists are in Dealey Plaza studying the area.

## FAST FACT

THE ZAPRUDER FILM WAS BOUGHT BY *LIFE* MAGAZINE FOR $150,000.

**To this day, conspiracy theorists leave Xs on the road where Kennedy was shot. The Texas School Book Depository can be seen in the background.**

In her interview, Pat described how it felt to see her city **portrayed** in this way:

*It was a very tough time for Dallas ... and we took quite a beating in the national press ... Dallas was very different then from what it is now. It was just a big country town ... It wasn't anywhere near as sophisticated or international as it is now. So it hurt that we all got labeled as radicals and so on.*

*Because we lived in Garland, we were a little bit removed from [the fear] ... Everything was locked down. You couldn't go anywhere or do anything, couldn't get in or out of town if you wanted to. I don't think there was really any fear in the*

**Kennedy's burial ceremony at Arlington National Cemetery is shown here.**

## FAST FACT

**THE TEXAS SCHOOL BOOK DEPOSITORY'S SIXTH FLOOR IS NOW A MUSEUM DEDICATED TO KENNEDY'S ASSASSINATION.**

*suburbs as much as there probably was in the down-town area where all that was taking place.*

Dallas became more than the location of a crime. It became a **symbol**, and for many residents of the city, the criticism felt personal, as if they were being blamed for something they hadn't caused nor supported.

## KENNEDY'S FUNERAL

Kennedy's funeral took place on November 25 and was one of the most widely watched and emotional events in American history. Hundreds of thousands gathered in Washington, D.C., to mourn in person, while millions more watched the footage on TV.

**Kennedy's casket was taken through Washington, D.C., on a horse-drawn cart.**

The funeral procession was carefully planned, with Jacqueline Kennedy modeling it after Abraham Lincoln's funeral. Kennedy's casket was carried by a horse-drawn cart, with a riderless black horse following it. Jacqueline Kennedy and her children, three-year-old John Jr. and five-year-old Caroline, walked behind the casket. John Jr. famously saluted his father's casket as it passed.

Kennedy was buried at Arlington National Cemetery, where an eternal flame was lit at his graveside. The flame has never

**One of the most famous pictures from John F. Kennedy's funeral is this one of his son saluting his casket as it went by him.**

**The eternal flame has never permanently gone out. It is shown here behind Kennedy's gravestone.**

permanently gone out, and some upgrades have been made over the years to ensure the flame always stays lit. In 2013, the Army Corps of Engineers upgraded the burner and gas lines to make it even more dependable in all weather conditions. There is also a flashing electric spark near the nozzle to reignite the gas if the flame goes out.

Kennedy's gravesite covers about 3.2 acres (1.2 ha) of ground in the cemetery. It is the final resting place for John F. Kennedy; Jacqueline, who died in 1994; and two infant children who had died shortly after being born.

## HOW YOU SEE HISTORY

1. Why do you think Jacqueline chose to model her husband's funeral after that of Abraham Lincoln?
2. Why do you think Dallas became a target of national criticism?
3. What responsibilities do news organizations have during a national crisis when the facts are still unclear?

# CHAPTER FIVE

# REMEMBERING JOHN F. KENNEDY

Kennedy's assassination continues to impact people even today. Conspiracy theories about the assassination are still discussed. It's influenced safety protocols to this day. And for those who witnessed the assassination in Dallas or tried to help Kennedy, like Secret Service Agent Clint Hill, the effects of being there have lasted decades. In Marna's interview, she discussed Clint Hill, her connection to him, and how not being able to save Kennedy continued to haunt him for many years.

## SECRET SERVICE AGENT CLINT HILL

Clint Hill was assigned to protect the Kennedys on November 22. As the motorcade moved through Dealey Plaza, he was right behind the president's car. When the shots rang out, he ran toward the moving vehicle, jumping onto the back and pushing Jacqueline Kennedy down into the seat as the car sped away. Throughout the entire drive to the hospital, Hill stayed on the back of the car to shield the First Lady. Yet for many years, he believed that he had failed.

Marna said in an interview that she knew Hill because he was a friend of her brother and had been in his wedding. She said:

*His job was so important to him and he felt so strongly that he*

**Scan this QR code to watch Marna talk about Secret Service Agent Clint Hill, who tried to save Kennedy.**

*was just filled with guilt because he had not saved the president. So for many years, in fact, just until the last couple years, Clint Hill was gone. He just dropped out, and his life just folded around him. And in the last couple years he's come back, he has co-authored a book, he was given a great award at his school, Concordia College.*

## FAST FACT

THE DAY OF KENNEDY'S FUNERAL, NOVEMBER 25TH, WAS ALSO THE DAY OF JOHN JR.'S BIRTHDAY. CAROLINE'S BIRTHDAY WAS TWO DAYS LATER.

**Secret Service Agent Clint Hill immediately jumped onto the back of the moving car to protect Jacqueline Kennedy.**

**Clint Hill is shown here at a book event in 2016. He died in 2025 at the age of 93.**

> **FAST FACT**
>
> A TAXI DRIVER IN THE AREA SAID THAT ON THE DAY OF KENNEDY'S FUNERAL, THE CROWDS WERE SO QUIET THAT A PIN COULD BE HEARD DROPPING.

Hill was overwhelmed by guilt. He believed if he reacted a moment sooner, if he was more **vigilant**, he may have saved Kennedy. For years, he withdrew from public life and rarely spoke about Dallas. He carried the weight of that day and watching the death of the president for many years.

**Kennedy's burial ceremony was attended by many people who personally knew him or just wanted to pay their respects.**

Eventually, he was able to write books about his experience. In 2012, he published a book with Lisa McCubbin called *Mrs. Kennedy and Me*, which was a behind-the-scenes look at the Kennedys' lives, and in 2013, he co-authored a book with McCubbin called *Five Days in November* about the assassination. Hill's story shows that healing from trauma can take decades.

## THE AFTERMATH OF KENNEDY'S DEATH

More than 60 years after his death, John F. Kennedy is still a powerful symbol in American history. Memorials to him can be found across the states, and an airport in New York City bears his name.

The Kennedy name is also defined by tragedy to this day. In 1968, John F. Kennedy's brother, Robert, was also assassinated. He was running for president that year and was speaking to supporters at the Ambassador Hotel in Los Angeles, California, when Sirhan Sirhan shot him three times at close range in the head and body.

**John F. Kennedy's brother, Robert (shown here) was assassinated just five years after his brother.**

Robert Kennedy died at the hospital the next day. In 1999, John F. Kennedy's son, John Jr., died in a plane crash along with his wife and sister-in-law. For many Americans, these events brought up the idea of the "Kennedy curse," which is often used to describe the family's repeated encounters with tragedy.

Kennedy's assassination remains one of the most shocking events in American history. It changed how the government approaches

# THE WARREN COMMISSION

After Kennedy was assassinated, the nation demanded answers. To investigate, President Lyndon B. Johnson established the President's Commission on the Assassination of President John F. Kennedy on November 29, 1963. This group became known as the Warren Commission, after the chairman, Chief Justice Earl Warren.

The purpose of the commission was to examine all evidence from the assassination, including witness testimonies, forensic reports, photographs, and films such as the Zapruder film. The goal was to determine how Kennedy was killed, Oswald's actions before and after the assassination, and whether anyone else was involved.

The investigation lasted nearly a year, releasing the final report in September 1964. It concluded that Oswald acted alone in killing Kennedy and there was no credible evidence of a conspiracy. The report also discussed Oswald's killing of Tippit after the assassination.

The Warren Commission was important because it was the first official, government-backed account of the assassination. Its intention was to provide clarity surrounding the assassination, but it ended up leading to more debates and theories. Many people questioned the findings and continue to believe that there was another shooter. This also led to later investigations like the House Select Committee on Assassinations (HSCA), which was started in 1976 to investigate Kennedy's assassination as well as the assassination of civil rights activist Martin Luther King Jr. in 1968. The committee found that Kennedy and King were likely assassinated as a result of conspiracies and that there may have been a second shooter and organized crime may have played a role in Kennedy's assassination.

**The Warren Commission investigators are shown here.**

**The tragedies of the Kennedy family entered the media again when John F. Kennedy Jr., shown here, died in a plane crash.**

## FAST FACT

ASSASSINATING A PRESIDENT WASN'T A FEDERAL CRIME WHEN KENNEDY WAS ASSASSINATED. IT WASN'T UNTIL 1965 THAT KILLING, KIDNAPPING, OR HARMING THE PRESIDENT, VICE PRESIDENT, OR SUCCESSORS BECAME A CRIME.

presidential security and how it responds to national crises. Kennedy led the country during a tense period of the Cold War. He supported civil rights, space exploration, and economic growth, all of which had incredible lasting effects on the country.

Even decades later, Kennedy's decisions as a pres-

**The Kennedy gravesite is shown here with the lit eternal flame in the background.**

ident as well as his assassination mark some of the most influential moments in U.S. history.

## HOW YOU SEE HISTORY

1. Do you think the role of Secret Service agents can be emotionally demanding? How might their work affect their lives years later?
2. Why do you think conspiracy theories still exist about Kennedy's assassination, even after the Warren Commission published its findings? Do you think the HSCA played a part in the continuation of conspiracy theories? Why or why not?
3. Why do you think the assassination of John F. Kennedy still fascinates Americans to this day?

# TIMELINE

## BEFORE THE ASSASSINATION: TIMELINE OF THE KENNEDY ASSASSINATION

**1960:** Kennedy wins the presidential election.

## THE DAY UNFOLDS: TIMELINE OF THE KENNEDY ASSASSINATION

**November 22, 1963:** The Kennedys arrive in Dallas in the morning.

**12:30 p.m.:** Lee Harvey Oswald fires three shots, hitting Kennedy in the head and neck and hitting Governor Connally in the back.

**1:00 p.m.:** Kennedy is declared dead.

**1:15 p.m.:** Oswald shoots and kills Patrolman J.D. Tippit.

**1:45 p.m.:** Oswald is seized by police.

**1:30 p.m., November 23, 1963:** Oswald is charged with murder.

**November 24, 1963:** Oswald is shot on live television and dies.

## THE TRANSFER OF POWER: TIMELINE OF THE KENNEDY ASSASSINATION

**2:38 p.m., November 22, 1963:** Vice President Lyndon B. Johnson is sworn in as president.

## THE WORLD REACTS: TIMELINE OF THE KENNEDY ASSASSINATION

**November 25, 1963:** Kennedy's funeral is held.

**1998:** The Zapruder film is held by the National Archives.

## REMEMBERING JOHN F. KENNEDY: TIMELINE OF THE KENNEDY ASSASSINATION

**November 29, 1963:** President Johnson starts the Warren Commission to investigate the assassination.

# GLOSSARY

**acquire:** To get or come into possession of something.

**arraign:** To formally bring someone who has been charged with a crime into court to hear the charges against them.

**artifact:** Something made by humans in the past that still exists.

**confiscate:** To take away.

**constituent:** A resident in an area who elects an official to represent them.

**contradict:** To say the opposite of something said previously.

**criticism:** Disapproval of someone or something based on believed mistakes.

**decoy:** Something used to move someone away from a real target.

**defect:** To leave a country or political party, often to join a rival.

**diplomacy:** Managing relations between countries or groups and using communication to resolve issues.

**dissolution:** The breaking of something into smaller parts.

**eliminate:** To put an end to or get rid of.

**integrity:** The state of being honest, trustworthy, and consistently doing the right thing.

**itinerary:** A plan of things to do.

**mingle:** To mix with others, often by talking with others at a social event.

**portray:** To represent or describe something.

**protocol:** An agreed-upon set of rules or procedures.

**proximity:** Being near to something else.

**reputation:** The views that are held about something or someone.

**seize:** To get or take something by force.

**stringent:** Very demanding, often applying to rules.

**symbol:** Something that stands for something else.

**traumatized:** Affected by something very shocking or upsetting.

**vigilant:** Very aware of one's surroundings.

# FOR MORE INFORMATION

## BOOKS

Bugliosi, Vincent. *Reclaiming History: The Assassination of President John F. Kennedy*. New York, NY: W.W. Norton & Company, 2007.

Dallek, Robert. *An Unfinished Life: John F. Kennedy*. New York, NY: Back Bay Books, 2003.

Hill, Clint, and Lisa McCubbin. *Five Days in November*. New York, NY: Gallery Books, 2014.

Swanson, James L. *"The President Has Been Shot!": The Assassination of John F. Kennedy*. New York, NY: Scholastic Press, 2013.

Willens, Howard P. *History Will Prove Us Right: Inside the Warren Commission Report on the Assassination of John F. Kennedy*. New York, NY: The Overlook Press, 2013.

## WEBSITES

**Assassination of John F. Kennedy**
*www.britannica.com/event/assassination-of-John-F-Kennedy/Kennedys-funeral*
Read in-depth information about the assassination and Kennedy's funeral.

**JFK.org**
*www.jfk.org/*
The website of the John F. Kennedy memorial in the Texas School Book Depository includes photos, an interactive timeline, and more.

**"The JFK Assassination: Former Agent Recalls His Role in the Investigation"**
*www.fbi.gov/news/stories/the-jfk-assassination-former-agent-recalls-his-role-in-the-investigation*
Read and watch an interview with a former FBI Special Agent, who was a part of the assassination investigation.

**John F. Kennedy Presidential Library and Museum**
*www.jfklibrary.org/*
Learn more about the life and assassination of John F. Kennedy at the website for his official presidential library.

**The President John F. Kennedy Assassination Records Collection**
*www.archives.gov/research/jfk*
Learn more about the assassination and Warren Commission through official transcripts collected by the National Archives.

# INDEX

# PHOTO CREDITS

Cover JFK limousine/Wikimedia Commons; p. 7 piemags/rmn/Alamy Photos; p. 9 Bill Waterson/Alamy Photos; p. 10 John F. Kennedy campaigning in Florida 1960/wikimedia Commons; p. 11 ClassicStock/Alamy Photos; p. 12 *Profiles in Courage* Front Cover (1956 first edition)/Wikimedia Commons; p. 13 CubaSites1962/Wikimedia Commons; p. 14 Kennedys arrive at Dallas 11-22-63/Wikimedia Commons; p. 16 Niday Picture Library/Alamy Photos; p. 17 Carlo Bollo/Alamy Photos; p. 18 Glasshouse Images/Alamy Photos; p. 20 President and Mrs Kennedy deplane from Air Force One (3083217259)/Wikimedia Commons; p. 21 Recall Pictures/Alamy Photos; p. 22 Alpha Historica/Alamy Photos; pp. 23, 46 Dennis MacDonald/Alamy Photos; pp. 24, 53 courtesy of the Library of Congress; p. 25 Bill Waterson/Alamy Photos; p. 26 Maurice Savage/Alamy Photos; p. 27 Jack Ruby 1963 Mugshot/Wikimedia Commons; p. 28 Roger Coulam/Alamy Photos; p. 29 Teresa Otto/Alamy Photos; p. 31 President JFK's casket is transferred to Air Force One at Dallas Love Field (05)/Wikimedia Commons; p. 32 TaurusPhotography/Alamy Photos; p. 33 JFK Presidential Library - Swearing-in ceremony aboard Air Force One LBJ as President (04)/Wikimedia Commons; p. 35 VASILIS VERVERIDIS/Alamy Photos; p. 38 American Photo Archive/Alamy Photos; p. 39 Body of JFK being placed on catafalque in East Room/Wikimedia Commons; p. 40 Zapruder Camera/Wikimedia Commons; p. 41 Jerome Cid/Alamy Photos; p. 42 Stephen Saks Photography/Alamy Photos; p. 43 AR8255-3L. Burial of President John F. Kennedy at Arlington National Cemetery/Wikimedia Commons; p. 44 Glasshouse Images/Alamy Photos; p. 45 Steve Skjold/Alamy Photos; p. 49 Clint Hill on the limousine/Wikimedia Commons; p. 50 WENN Rights Ltd/Alamy Photos; p. 51 AR8255-2X. Burial of President John F. Kennedy at Arlington National Cemetery/Wikimedia Commons; p. 52 Archive PL/Alamy Photos; p. 54 CelebrityArchaeology.com/Alamy Photos; p. 55 Robertharding/Alamy Photos.

# ABOUT THE AUTHOR

**NICOLE HORNING** is a published author of several nonfiction books for children and teens. She has her Bachelor's degree in English and a Master's degree in education. She doesn't just write for a living; she also enjoys it as a hobby. Nicole loves to collect books and read anything that sounds interesting to her. She also loves learning new things, especially historical topics. She does her best work while listening to Taylor Swift and having one of her two cats in her lap—both things happen a lot.